50 SHADES of FUN

The New Joy of Coloring
and Law of Attraction Journaling

Pamela Thompson

Focus on Your Success LLC

50 Shades of Fun:
The New Joy of Coloring and Law of Attraction Journaling

© 2015 by Pamela Thompson,
Focus on Your Success LLC

Published by Focus on Your Success LLC
ISBN-13: 978-0692518557/ ISBN-10: 069251855X

To learn more about the Law of Attraction,
please visit my website at FocusOnYourSuccess.com

Since you purchased this book, be sure to join my Facebook Page,
"50 Shades of Fun: The New Joy of Coloring," so you can
download monthly bonus coloring pages.

Please visit my Etsy store, FocusonFunNow, for more
unique coloring pages, coloring greeting cards,
and post cards for your enjoyment.

Contact Pamela Thompson directly at (972) 832-5600

Cover Design – Co-creative effort: inspired by Source, and designed and created by
June Holzwarth, who can be contacted directly (June, not Source)
through LinkedIn.com or at (203) 385-3432

Editing and Formatting – Donna Hawkins, donnadelayed@hotmail.com

I am dedicating this book to
my Daughters – Monica Robinson and Chelsea Collins –
they are both coloring enthusiasts, and I appreciate
their love of my artwork and their encouragement.

Why "Law of Attraction" and Coloring?

I began studying the Law of Attraction (LOA) in 2005. As a result, I learned how important it is to be clear about what I choose to enjoy, and how to maintain a positive attitude most of the time. I learned this and more from Abraham-Hicks[1], and many others who have followed their own passion to learn more and share, just as I'm doing now. I am eternally grateful to Esther and Jerry Hicks for their willingness to co-create with us, sharing Abraham's infinite intelligence and pure positive energy with all who are a match to hearing. Many of the LOA-inspired thoughts herein are directly inspired by Abraham.

The Law of Attraction is a Universal Law that affects our lives, whether we acknowledge it or not, just as the Law of Gravity does. Most of us have been conditioned to react to everything around us, rather than being proactive by choosing how to feel and behave. In other words, we create *by default*, rather than *by intent*. In order to *deliberately* create the *joyful* lives we desire, we need to know how to *deliberately* harness the power of the Law of Attraction. Abraham suggests "Segment Intending" to pre-pave each new "segment" of your day, with a deliberate focus on a positive outcome.

If you are relatively new to the Law of Attraction, I urge you to check out the *Five Steps to Feel Better* workbook, a free download on my website, *FocusonYourSuccess.com*. This will help you clarify what you're asking for, making it easier to focus on it positively. It will also familiarize you with some of the techniques I share in the LOA-inspired thoughts contained herein.

These are the 3 Steps to using the Law of Attraction *deliberately*:

1. <u>Ask</u> – You already do this all of the time, often without realizing it. Any time you have a desire, you are asking.

---

[1] Visit abraham-hicks.com for more information about the Law of Attraction.

2. <u>Answer</u> – The Universe … Source … God … your Inner Being … whomever you consider your Higher Power … "hears" your thoughts vibrationally, and makes the object of your desire available to you.

3. <u>Allow Yourself to Receive</u> – This is your responsibility. You must allow yourself to emotionally match your desire in order to attract it. It's your job to feel as happy as if you've already attracted what you wish to be, do, or have.

Our thoughts vibrate on frequencies, just like sound waves and radio waves. Our emotions tell us whether our thoughts are vibrating positively or negatively. In other words, they tell us what we're attracting. There are many ways to become an emotional match to your desires – expressing gratitude, focusing specifically on how you choose to feel using visualization, making manifestation boards with pictures or words representing what you want, meditating, and just plain having fun – these and others will allow you to attract more of everything that feels good to you, since they will positively raise your vibration.

I've found, and many others seem to agree, that coloring detailed pictures, patterns, or mandalas is FUN, and it has proven to be as beneficial as meditation. In a recent HuffPost Live video interview online,[2] clinical psychologist Ben Michaelis, Ph.D. said coloring is something he "absolutely supports for mental health," and that it's "absolutely another form of meditation." He explained that engaging in a repetitive action helps you *release* whatever you're focusing on. This activates certain parts of your mind that involve a higher consciousness. By allowing your mind to work in a *different* way, you will find it easier to shift your perspective to one that feels better.

It makes sense. And, while it may be difficult to quiet your thoughts on your own, it's easy to attain a meditative state while coloring. Any time you indulge in something you enjoy, you literally get lost in the fun of it. And, coloring can spark creativity, even if you never

---

[2] *Why Coloring is a Beneficial Stress Relief,* HuffPost Live, July 27, 2015, http://live.huffingtonpost.com/r/segment/coloring-adults-stress/55af7fb1fe34445cec000185

even considered yourself creative. *Now, you can use coloring as a way to spark the creation of anything you desire, as you learn to use the Law of Attraction to your benefit.*

The many Law of Attraction-inspired thoughts and suggestions in this book are intended to help you create a more positive focus. I wish to encourage uplifting journaling – writing gratitude lists, listing positive qualities of people, things, or situations, describing your life the way you want it to be – these techniques create the positive momentum necessary to attract more good into your life.

There is no exclusion with the Law of Attraction; you always get what you focus on. If you find yourself focusing primarily on negativity, the Law of Attraction will work to bring you more to feel badly about. So, if you say "I'm sick of being broke," you are setting yourself up for more situations that match that negative feeling. Wouldn't it feel better to say "I choose to be financially secure and at ease?" Try focusing more positively with your statements, and watch what happens.

I wish you many hours of ease and fun while coloring these pages. Just flip through the book and stop at an illustration that feels right for you at that moment. You may be pleasantly surprised that the thoughts before and after that drawing hold a suggestion that puts you at ease or provides guidance about something that has been on your mind.

The blank pages in this book are intentional to protect the journal pages from coloring bleed through. If you choose to use colored pencils, Crayola Twisters, or other pens that do not bleed through, there are many ways to take advantage of these blank pages. Some suggestions are to use them as additional journal pages to write gratitude lists, or positive aspects of people, places, or situations, or to write the story of your life the way you intend it to be. You can also draw some of your own illustrations – coloring often brings out creativity in us that we never realized was there.

Please feel free to share your creations on my Facebook page, *50 Shades of Fun: The New Joy of Coloring,* for everyone to enjoy!

HAVE FUN COLORING!

If what you are thinking about feels bad, think about something else – anything else that feels better.

_____

_____

_____

_____

_____

_____

_____

_____

_____

_____

_____

Make a mental list of all the things
that are going well in your life.

If you focus on something that feels bad – think about it, talk about it, worry about it – you basically go to a negative place on purpose!

_____

_____

_____

_____

_____

_____

_____

_____

_____

_____

_____

Try telling a better-feeling story instead. Focus on what would feel good to you. Start by saying, "Wouldn't it be nice if . . . ."

Take the time to imagine, visualize, and feel the outcomes you want for upcoming events in your life. Act as if they have already happened in ways that are pleasing to you.

_____

_____

_____

_____

_____

_____

_____

_____

_____

_____

When you focus on what you desire with a positive attitude, you attract positive outcomes.

We came into these physical bodies to experience variety, and to create and expand because of it.

It's wonderful that we have so much control
over everything we desire and create,
no matter how big or small it is.

There are no exceptions with the Law of Attraction; you get what you focus on.

_____

_____

_____

_____

_____

_____

_____

_____

_____

_____

_____

Instead of repeating what you don't want,
focus in a positive manner on exactly
what you choose to experience.

No one else came into his or her physical body for the purpose of pleasing you. It's your job to please yourself.

_____

_____

_____

_____

_____

_____

_____

_____

_____

_____

_____

When you find joy daily, you'll attract more people and experiences that feel good, and others won't have to behave differently to make you happy.

Passion is one of the most important things to have; it fuels dreams, desires, and all of creation.

_____

_____

_____

_____

_____

_____

_____

_____

_____

_____

_____

When you think about, talk about, and
dream about your passions, you are aligned with
pure positive energy.

If you see others struggling, trust that they are on their own journeys of expansion.

_____

_____

_____

_____

_____

_____

_____

_____

_____

_____

_____

_____

Focus on them finding peace and ease in their lives.

Acknowledge all the wonderful things you presently enjoy in your life. Simply look around from where you are sitting right now.

_____

_____

_____

_____

_____

_____

_____

_____

_____

_____

_____

When you allow yourself to appreciate everything,
big and small, you attract more
wonderful things in your life.

Success doesn't bring happiness.
Happiness brings success.

When you take the time to have fun every day,
your desires are fulfilled with greater ease.

Let go of your regrets. Don't dwell on them, talk about them, worry about them, or defend yourself.

_____

_____

_____

_____

_____

_____

_____

_____

_____

_____

_____

_____

You can start right now to improve any situation
in your life, simply by focusing on the solution
and how you choose to feel.

You are Source, you are eternal, and you are very powerful.

_____

_____

_____

_____

_____

_____

_____

_____

_____

_____

_____

Take credit for your positive decision
to live in the physical – you created YOU!
How awesome is that!!?

When the step you're about to take feels like a "Hell YES!" you've made the right choice.

_____

_____

_____

_____

_____

_____

_____

_____

_____

_____

_____

_____

There are only two kinds of emotions, good-feeling ones and bad-feeling ones. Listen to them! If something feels good, do it. If it feels bad, stop.

There is plenty of everything in our Universe. You can be, do, or have everything you want.

_____

_____

_____

_____

_____

_____

_____

_____

_____

_____

_____

All you have to do is stay as happy as possible, and know that whatever you desire is on its way.

You would never want all of your desires to appear at once. You couldn't possibly enjoy them all at once.

_____

_____

_____

_____

_____

_____

_____

_____

_____

_____

_____

_____

Enjoy the anticipation, appreciate the
"tweaking time." Then, experience
your magnificent creation in awe.

We came into this physical life intending to face variety and contrast, to help us decide what we prefer to create. This is how we expand.

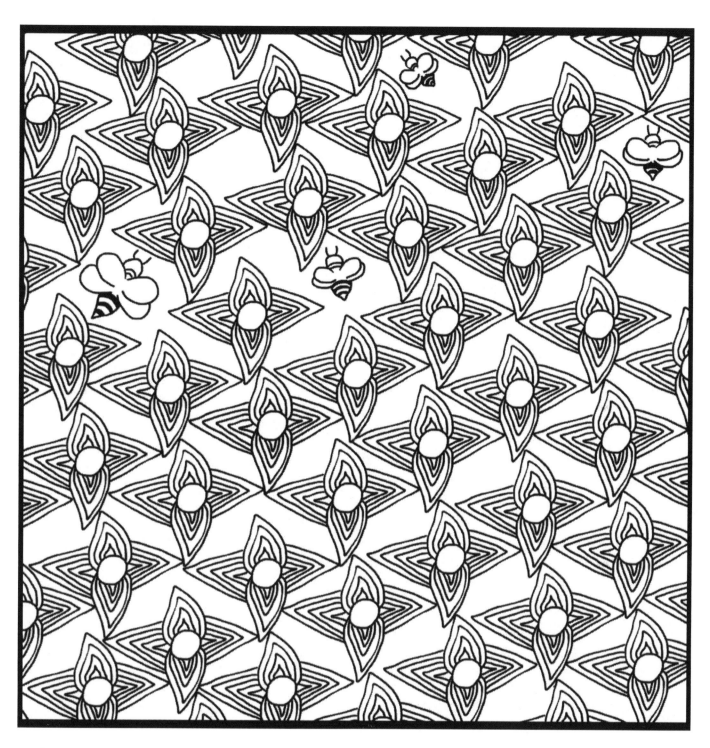

We will never get it all done, because we are eternal. Once goals are attained, we come up with new desires – that's what makes life so much fun!

Brainstorm about things you'd like to have, be, or do. Think outside the box. Don't try to figure out the "how" – the Universe will show you the way.

_____

_____

_____

_____

_____

_____

_____

_____

_____

_____

_____

Life is supposed to be fun, so relax and
enjoy yourself in every possible moment.

We can't control others, or create their reality – only they have that power.

_____

_____

_____

_____

_____

_____

_____

_____

_____

_____

_____

_____

We are each on our own personal journey
of expansion, and we can only hear
what we are a match to hearing.

You, and only you, control your thoughts.
Therefore, you, and only you,
control your experiences.

_____

_____

_____

_____

_____

_____

_____

_____

_____

_____

_____

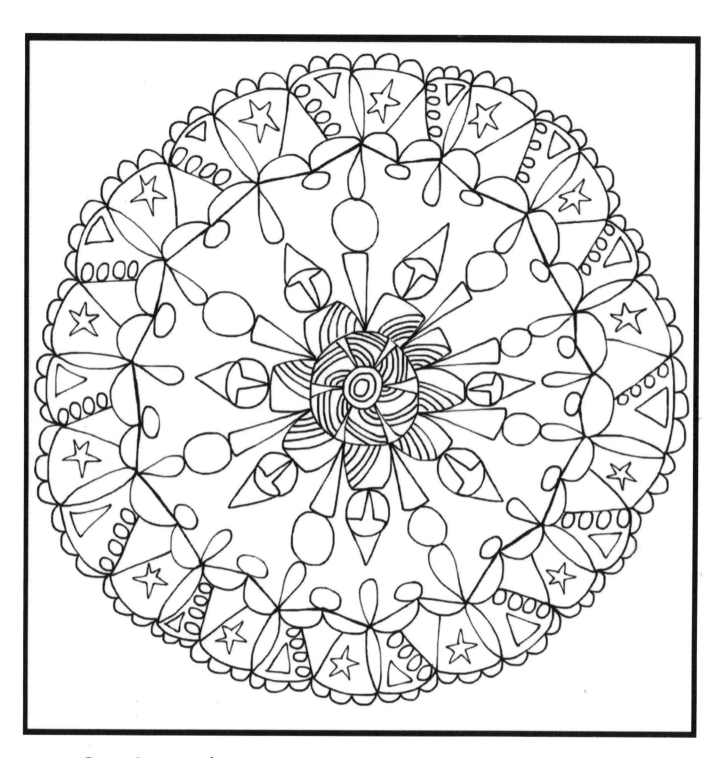

Be clear about what you wish to experience.
Use Segment Intending throughout the day
to set yourself up for success.

The Universe is infinitely abundant.
Focus on all the abundance you presently enjoy.

_____

_____

_____

_____

_____

_____

_____

_____

_____

_____

_____

_____

List everything you are grateful to have in abundance today. Focus on whatever feels good – love, friends, books, paper, clothes – anything!

We are all responsible for our own happiness; do something fun today!

_____

_____

_____

_____

_____

_____

_____

_____

_____

_____

_____

_____

Think about things you've always wanted, and imagine how much fun they will be. Don't worry about how – the Universe will show you.

Every relationship will thrive with ease when freedom is allowed.

_____

_____

_____

_____

_____

_____

_____

_____

_____

_____

_____

You came to create a joyful life for yourself.
Allow others to do the same in their own ways.

Be as happy about spending money as you are about attracting it; then more will flow to you.

_____

_____

_____

_____

_____

_____

_____

_____

_____

_____

_____

Every time you spend money, you are helping
someone else somewhere. How wonderful is that?

Whether seeking a life partner or an improved relationship, it's important to be happy with yourself first.

_____

_____

_____

_____

_____

_____

_____

_____

_____

_____

Declare to your loved ones that you don't hold them responsible for your happiness, and you are not responsible for theirs.

Worry is using your imagination to create what you don't want.

_____

_____

_____

_____

_____

_____

_____

_____

_____

_____

_____

When faced with a challenging situation, imagine a positive outcome. Think only good thoughts, and watch as wonderful things unfold.

Do something different today for fun – try a new recipe, call an old friend, draw a picture, sing a song, or take a walk.

_____

_____

_____

_____

_____

_____

_____

_____

_____

_____

_____

Appreciate the freedom of choice you have during your free time.

Make a list of all your positive qualities.
Read it aloud daily, with feeling,
to yourself in the mirror for a couple weeks.

_____

_____

_____

_____

_____

_____

_____

_____

_____

_____

_____

It's wonderful to validate yourself. Then, compliments from others are just icing on the cake!

Happiness is a choice! Own your power to be happy regardless of others.

_____

_____

_____

_____

_____

_____

_____

_____

_____

_____

_____

_____

You are not here to please anyone,
and no one is here to please you.

If you desire acceptance, set an example by accepting others, unconditionally.

_____

_____

_____

_____

_____

_____

_____

_____

_____

_____

_____

Everyone is on his or her own journey for joy.

There is something positive to be found in every person or situation.

_____

_____

_____

_____

_____

_____

_____

_____

_____

_____

_____

_____

There is no "right or wrong."
There are merely contrasting perspectives that help us become clearer about what we desire.

Your thoughts and feelings create your reality; focus clearly on what you desire.

_____

_____

_____

_____

_____

_____

_____

_____

_____

_____

_____

_____

_____

If you believe you can do it, and allow yourself
to feel it, you will attract the way.

Be clear about what you want, and imagine the emotions you will feel. Then, paying attention to Universal nudges, take action.

_____

_____

_____

_____

_____

_____

_____

_____

_____

_____

_____

_____

When you take Universe-inspired action, your goals will come into fruition with ease.

You only have the power to change yourself.
Focus on the kind of person you choose to be,
and how you choose to feel.

_____

_____

_____

_____

_____

_____

_____

_____

_____

_____

_____

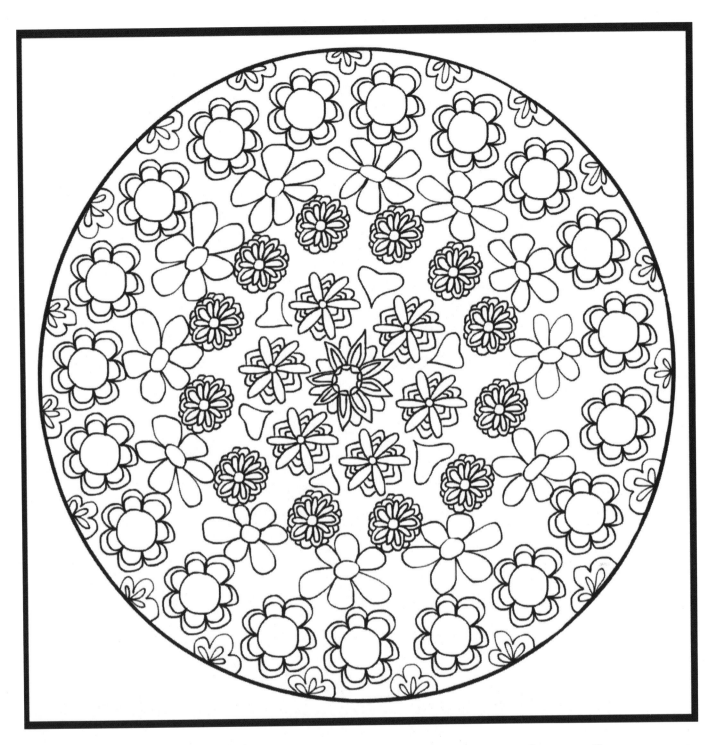

What qualities do you enjoy in others?
Create those in yourself first, and you'll attract
people with those qualities with greater ease.

By watching news or violent shows, you allow others to dump negativity into your lap, and give you a warped view of our wonderful world.

_____

_____

_____

_____

_____

_____

_____

_____

_____

_____

_____

_____

Our world really is full of loving people, beautiful places, and extraordinary circumstances.

The most important thing you can do is be happy.

_____

_____

_____

_____

_____

_____

_____

_____

_____

_____

_____

_____

_____

Start and end every day focusing on
what you are grateful for.

Never, ever, downplay your success, abundance, health, or confidence in your power to create your desires.

_____

_____

_____

_____

_____

_____

_____

_____

_____

_____

_____

_____

Complaining just adds fuel to the fire of
negativity, and attracts more of the same.
Be a positive inspiration, instead.

You control your thoughts, they determine how you feel, and your feelings indicate your vibration, to which Law of Attraction responds.

_____

_____

_____

_____

_____

_____

_____

_____

_____

_____

_____

_____

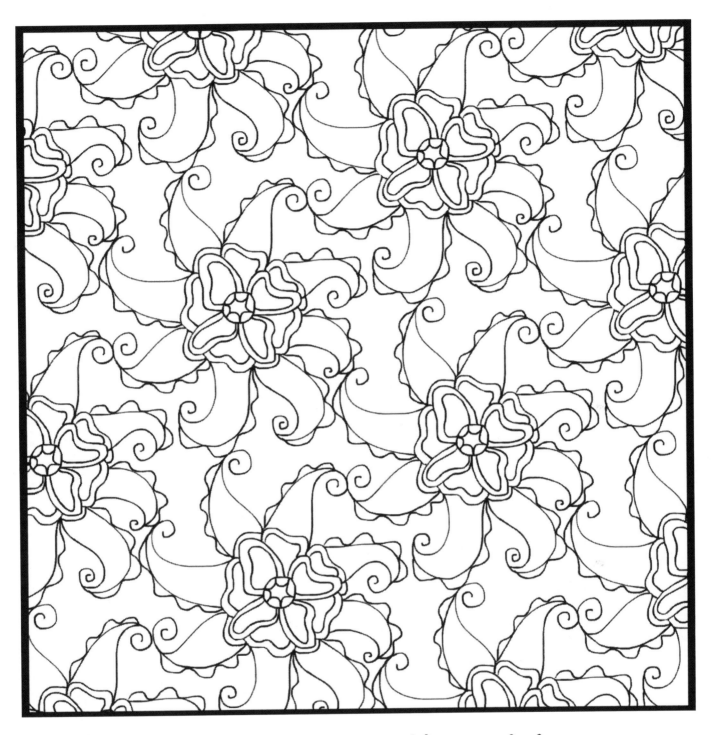

Choose your thoughts, deliberately keeping them positive and hopeful. The Universe will match your positive vibration.

The happier you are, the healthier you are.

_____

_____

_____

_____

_____

_____

_____

_____

_____

_____

_____

_____

Coloring is an excellent way to feel ease and have fun. So, here's to good health!

You always get the essence of what you focus on.

_____

_____

_____

_____

_____

_____

_____

_____

_____

_____

_____

_____

_____

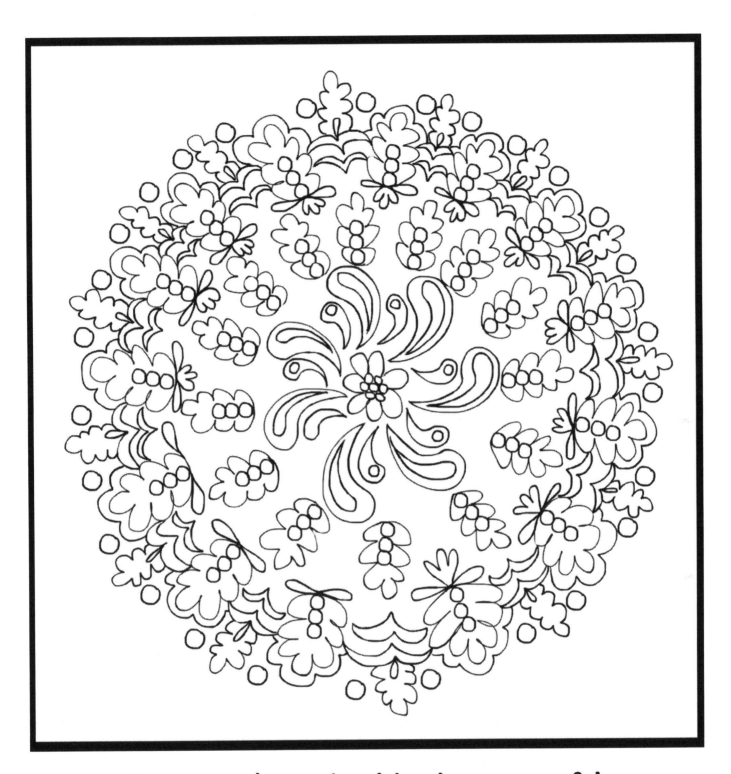

Focus on being healthy, happy, joyful,
and inspiring to others.

Meditation is very beneficial; it enables you to be aligned with pure positive energy.

_____

_____

_____

_____

_____

_____

_____

_____

_____

_____

_____

_____

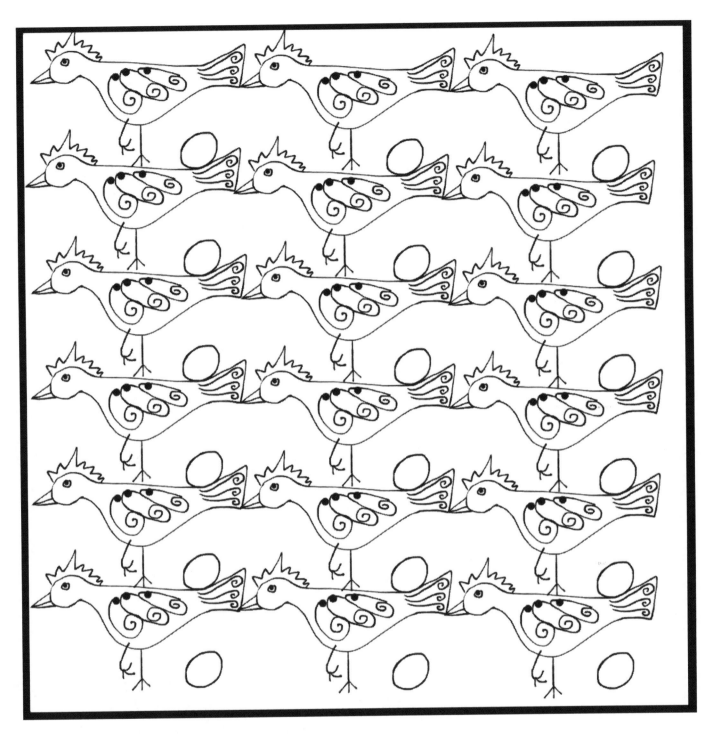

Writing Gratitude Lists and coloring have
the same benefits as meditation.

You have the power to let the past go; enjoy the present, and create your desired future.

_____

_____

_____

_____

_____

_____

_____

_____

_____

_____

_____

_____

No one is here to please you;
make it your business to please yourself.

We are all eternal. We have time for everything, so relax.

_____

_____

_____

_____

_____

_____

_____

_____

_____

_____

_____

Be easy on yourself. Inspired action is
much more productive than taking action
just because you think you should.

Start off every day, before you even get out of bed, with positive thoughts.

_____

_____

_____

_____

_____

_____

_____

_____

_____

_____

_____

_____

_____

It only takes 68 seconds of positive thoughts to build positive momentum and create pleasing outcomes throughout the day! Try it.

You cannot stop your thoughts from vibrating, and the Law of Attraction will never stop responding to the vibration you are offering.

Be deliberate about your thoughts and feelings,
as they determine how you are vibrating
and what you're attracting.

It doesn't matter what others think of you; what's important is how you feel about them.

_____

_____

_____

_____

_____

_____

_____

_____

_____

_____

_____

_____

When you love others unconditionally,
you attract more loving behavior from them.

If the reality you are experiencing stinks,
stop focusing on it, and start creating
the reality you want instead.

_____

_____

_____

_____

_____

_____

_____

_____

_____

_____

_____

_____

Be clear about what you desire, talk about it,
tell stories about it as if it has already happened,
and be grateful for it.

Life is full of variety, which is wonderful because the contrast makes us clearer about what we really want.

_____

_____

_____

_____

_____

_____

_____

_____

_____

_____

_____

_____

Learn to appreciate the differences for helping you
re-focus your thoughts on exactly what you choose
to enjoy or the person you choose to be.

Your emotions affect how you feel physically.

_____

_____

_____

_____

_____

_____

_____

_____

_____

_____

_____

_____

A healthy body is the result of a happy life.
What's working well in your body today?

Ignore reality. Tell your story – past, present, and future – the way you desire it to be. You are the director of your life.

_____

_____

_____

_____

_____

_____

_____

_____

_____

_____

_____

What would you like your relationship to be like?
Your childhood? Your job? Your health?
Your future? Write your own script.

Every time you ask for something, the Universe orchestrates everything necessary to satisfy your desire.

Your thoughts must be vibrating positively to attract all that you desire. That is why the most important thing you can do is be happy!

Made in the USA
San Bernardino, CA
17 January 2017